SACREDSPACE
for Lent 2009

SACREDSPACE

for Lent 2009

from the web site www.sacredspace.ie

Jesuit Communication Centre, Ireland

ave maria press AMP notre dame, indiana

acknowledgment

The publisher would like to thank Alan McGuckian, S.J., Gerry Bourke, S.J., and Piaras Jackson, S.J., for their kind assistance in making this book possible. Correspondence with the Sacred Space team can be directed to feedback@ sacredspace.ie. Piaras Jackson, S.J., Gerry Bourke, S.J., Paul Andrews, S.J., and John McDermott welcome all comments on the material or on the site.

Unless otherwise noted, the Scripture quotations contained herein are from the *New Revised Standard Version Bible*, copyright © 1989 by the Division of Christian Education of the National Council of the Churches of Christ in the United States of America. Used by permission. All rights reserved.

Published under license from Michelle Anderson Publishing Pty Ltd., in Australia

Founded in 1865, Ave Maria Press is a ministry of the Indiana Province of Holy Cross.

www.avemariapress.com

ISBN-10: 1-59471-181-X   ISBN-13: 978-1-59471-181-7

Cover and text design by K. H. Coney.

Printed and bound in the United States of America.

how to use this book

During this Lenten season, we invite you to make a sacred space in your day. Spend ten minutes praying here and now, wherever you are, with the help of a prayer guide and scripture chosen specially for each day. Every place is a sacred space, so you may wish to have this little book available at any time or place during the course of the day . . . in your desk at work, while traveling, on your bedside table, in your purse or jacket pocket . . . . Remember that God is everywhere, all around us, constantly reaching out to us, even in the most unlikely situations. When we know this, and with a bit of practice, we can pray anywhere.

The following pages will guide you through a session of prayer stages.

Something to think and pray about each day
  this week

The Presence of God

Freedom

Consciousness

The Word (leads you to the daily Lenten scripture and provides help with the text)

Conversation

Conclusion

It is most important to come back to these pages each day of the week as they are an integral part of each day's prayer and lead to the scripture and inspiration points.

Although written in the first person, the prayers are for "doing" rather than for reading out. Each stage is a kind of exercise or mediation aimed at helping you to get in touch with God and God's presence in your life.

We hope that you will join the many people around the world praying with us in our sacred space.

The Presence of God

Bless all who worship you, almighty God,
from the rising of the sun to its setting:
from your goodness enrich us,
by your love inspire us,
by your Spirit guide us,
by your power protect us,
in your mercy receive us,
now and always.

Something to think and pray about each day this week:

Getting Started

We are starting Lent this week, a somber time.

You did not come, O God, to judge us, but to seek what is lost, to set free those who are imprisoned in guilt and fear, and to save us when our hearts accuse us. Take us as we are, with all that sinful past of the world. You are greater than our hearts, and greater than all our guilt—you are the creator of a new future, and a God of Love forever and ever.

The Presence of God
At any time of the day or night
we can call on Jesus.
He is always waiting,
listening for our call.
What a wonderful blessing!
No phone needed, no e-mails,
just a whisper.

Freedom
I will ask God's help,
to be free from my own preoccupations,
to be open to God in this time of prayer,
to come to love and serve him more.

Consciousness
How am I really feeling?
Light-hearted? Heavy-hearted?
I may be very much at peace,
happy to be here.

Equally, I may be frustrated,
worried or angry.
I acknowledge how I really am.
It is the real me that the Lord loves.

The Word

I read the Word of God slowly, a few times
over, and I listen to what God is saying to me.
(Please turn to your scripture on the following
pages. Inspiration points are there should you
need them. When you are ready, return here to
continue.)

Conversation

Remembering that I am
still in God's presence,
I imagine Jesus himself sitting beside me,
and say whatever is on my mind,
whatever is in my heart,
speaking as one friend to another.

Conclusion

Glory be to the Father, and to the Son, and
to the Holy Spirit, as it was in the beginning,
is now and ever shall be, world without end.
Amen.

Wednesday 25th February,
Ash Wednesday   Joel 2:12–14

Yet even now, says the Lord, return to me with all your heart, with fasting, with weeping, and with mourning; rend your hearts and not your clothing. Return to the Lord, your God, for he is gracious and merciful, slow to anger, and abounding in steadfast love, and relents from punishing. Who knows whether he will not turn and relent, and leave a blessing behind him, a grain offering and a drink offering for the Lord, your God?

- We are at that time of the year when we are invited to test our inner freedom and to question the notion: *I can take it, or leave it.* Try that with pornography, alcohol, complaining, gossiping, anger, gambling. What habits make me hard to live with?

- Lent is about regaining self-control, especially in those areas that damage others. We don't admire those whose appetites or habits lead them by the nose. *A pure heart create for me, O God. Put a steadfast spirit within me.*

Thursday 26th February

Deuteronomy 30:15–16,19–20

See, I have set before you today life and prosperity, death and adversity. If you obey the commandments of the Lord your God that I am commanding you today, by loving the Lord your God, walking in his ways, and observing his commandments, decrees, and ordinances, then you shall live and become numerous, and the Lord your God will bless you in the land that you are entering to possess. . . . Choose life so that you and your descendants may live, loving the Lord your God, obeying him, and holding fast to him; for that means life to you and length of days, so that you may live in the land that the Lord swore to give to your ancestors, to Abraham, to Isaac, and to Jacob.

- Today, Lord, you remind me that it is a small profit to gain the whole world if I lose my own soul. Today you set before me life and good, death and evil.

- Can I use this Lent to make more choices that are life-giving?

Friday 27th February   **Isaiah 58:5–9**

Is such the fast that I choose, a day to humble oneself? Is it to bow down the head like a bulrush, and to lie in sackcloth and ashes? Will you call this a fast, a day acceptable to the Lord? Is not this the fast that I choose: to loose the bonds of injustice, to undo the thongs of the yoke, to let the oppressed go free, and to break every yoke? Is it not to share your bread with the hungry,

and bring the homeless poor into your house;
when you see the naked, to cover them, and not
to hide yourself from your own kin? Then your
light shall break forth like the dawn, and your
healing shall spring up quickly; your vindicator
shall go before you, the glory of the Lord shall
be your rear guard. Then you shall call, and the
Lord will answer; you shall cry for help, and he
will say, Here I am.

- "Is not this the fast that I choose," says the Lord,
". . . to share your bread with the hungry, and
bring the homeless poor into your house? . . .
Then you shall call, and the Lord will answer."

- Lord, I am looking for a change in myself this
Lent. Help me to find the sort of generosity of
which you speak.

Saturday 28th February   Luke 5:27–32

After this he went out and saw a tax collector named Levi, sitting at the tax booth; and he said to him, "Follow me." And he got up, left everything, and followed him. Then Levi gave a great banquet for him in his house; and there was a large crowd of tax collectors and others sitting at the table with them. The Pharisees and their scribes were complaining to his disciples, saying, "Why do you eat and drink with tax collectors and sinners?" Jesus answered, "Those who are well have no need of a physician, but those who are sick; I have come to call not the righteous but sinners to repentance."

- In Caravaggio's painting of the call of Levi, the tax-collector is stunned and incredulous when he sees the beckoning finger of Jesus: *Who? Me! There must be some mistake!* But Jesus knew this man. Levi left everything, his cash-filled table and his moneyed friends, and followed the Lord.

The grace of God's call is free, but not cheap. A change of life is required.

• Jesus, may I share your feast, answer your call, and change my life.

Something to think and pray about each day this week:

Growing Pains

Lent reflects the rhythm of our spiritual life, between Tabor and Gethsemane, the Transfiguration and the Agony in the Garden. There are times when God shows himself, as on Tabor: prayer is easy, our hearts are light. We feel loved and loving, on holy ground. J.D. Salinger wrote: "All we do our whole lives is go from one little piece of Holy Ground to the next."

Then there are times of disagreeable growth. You remember the parable of the barren fig-tree (Luke 13:6), and the farmer who said: "I need a year to dig around it and manure it." We can feel God doing this to us, feel the pain when our roots are struck by the spade. We feel useless, past our best, no good to anyone, a failure in the most important things we have tried, whether marriage, vocation, rearing children, or our job and career. Life loses its savor. We cannot pray. We sense that some people think the world would be better off without us.

St. Ignatius called this state "desolation," and he advised: "Remember that it will pass . . . In consolation, think about how you will conduct yourself in time of desolation. And insist more on prayer." Then you come to see—gradually— that this same ground, however stinking, is holy, and you can find God there. He is wielding the spade, spreading the dung.

The Presence of God

For a few moments, I think of
God's veiled presence in things:
in the elements, giving them existence;
in plants, giving them life;
in animals, giving them sensation;
and finally, in me, giving me
all this and more, making me a temple,
a dwelling-place of the Spirit.

Freedom

God is not foreign to my freedom.
Instead, the Spirit breathes life
into my most intimate desires,
gently nudging me toward all that is good.
I ask for the grace to let myself
be enfolded by the Spirit.

Consciousness

Knowing that God loves me unconditionally,
I can afford to be honest about how I am.

How has the last day been,
and how do I feel now?
I share my feelings openly with the Lord.

The Word
The Word of God comes down to us through
the scriptures. May the Holy Spirit enlighten
my mind and my heart to respond to the gospel
teachings. (Please turn to your scripture on the
following pages. Inspiration points are there
should you need them. When you are ready, return here to continue.)

Conversation
How has God's Word moved me?
Has it left me cold?
Has it consoled me,
or moved me to act in a new way?
I imagine Jesus sitting beside me,
I turn and share my feelings with him.

Conclusion

Glory be to the Father, and to the Son, and to the Holy Spirit, as it was in the beginning, is now and ever shall be, world without end. Amen.

Sunday 1st March,
First Sunday of Lent Mark 1:12–15

A nd the Spirit immediately drove him out into the wilderness. He was in the wilderness forty days, tempted by Satan; and he was with the wild beasts; and the angels waited on him. Now after John was arrested, Jesus came to Galilee, proclaiming the Good News of God, and saying, "The time is fulfilled, and the Kingdom of God has come near; repent, and believe in the Good News."

- There is a time for every activity under the sun— a time to act and a time to pray.

- Sometimes the need is to act, and God calls me to go out and do something.

- At other times, I just need to spend time alone with God, and that will give me the strength and the wisdom to do the right thing when it is the time for doing.

- Can I speak to the Lord and ask him where he is calling me now?

Monday 2nd March   Matthew 25:34–40

Jesus said to his disciples, "Then the king will say to those at his right hand, 'Come, you that are blessed by my Father, inherit the kingdom prepared for you from the foundation of the world; for I was hungry and you gave me food, I was thirsty and you gave me something to drink, I was a stranger and you welcomed me, I was naked and you gave me clothing, I was sick and you took care of me, I was in prison and you visited me.' Then the righteous will answer him, 'Lord, when was it that we saw you hungry and gave you food, or thirsty and gave you something to drink? And when was it that we saw you a stranger and welcomed you, or naked and gave you clothing? And when was it that we saw you sick or in prison and visited you?' And the king will answer them,

'Truly I tell you, just as you did it to one of the least of these who are members of my family, you did it to me.'"

- Jesus challenges us to put our treatment of other people on par with our treatment of him.

- It is said that you can judge a society by the way it treats its weakest members. Jesus tells me I too can judge myself by the way I treat "the least" of people I meet.

- How do I feel when I hear this? Disbelieving? Guilty? Inspired? Challenged? Can I talk to the Lord about it?

- When I meet people today, can I treat them as I would treat Jesus?

Tuesday 3rd March   **Isaiah 55:10–12**

For as the rain and the snow come down from heaven, and do not return there until they have watered the earth, making it bring forth and sprout, giving seed to the sower and bread to the eater, so shall my word be that goes out from my mouth; it shall not return to me empty, but it shall accomplish that which I purpose, and succeed in the thing for which I sent it. For you shall go out in joy, and be led back in peace; the mountains and the hills before you shall burst into song, and all the trees of the field shall clap their hands.

- Isaiah has no doubt about the strength of purpose behind everything that God does and God's confidence that this purpose will be fulfilled.

- What purpose does God have for me? What does God want me to accomplish? Can I talk to the Lord about this?

- Transforming the world through love may sound like an ambitious mission to be a part of. Am I daunted by it? Can I ask the Lord for the grace of confidence and hope, for the kind of joy that Isaiah describes in this passage?

Wednesday 4th March
Psalm 51:1–3, 10–11, 16–17

Have mercy on me, O God, according to your steadfast love; according to your abundant mercy blot out my transgressions. Wash me thoroughly from my iniquity, and cleanse me from my sin. For I know my transgressions, and my sin is ever before me. . . . Create in me a clean heart, O God, and put a new and right spirit within me. Do not cast me away from your presence, and do not take your holy spirit from me. . . . For you have no delight in sacrifice; if I were to give a burnt offering, you would not be pleased. The sacrifice acceptable to God is a broken spirit; a broken and contrite heart, O God, you will not despise.

- "A broken and contrite heart, O God, you will not despise." Save me, Lord, from a religious hysteria that blinds me to the uglier side of myself. I want not merely to acknowledge the truth about my own sins, but also to keep a habitual sense of my weakness, which may save me from arrogance.

- I pray with St. Francis de Sales: *It is good to have a crevice in the soul and fill it with repentance; then you can grow there any virtue you please.*

Thursday 5th March   Matthew 7:7–11

Jesus said to the crowds, "Ask, and it will be given you; search, and you will find; knock, and the door will be opened for you. For everyone who asks receives, and everyone who searches finds, and for everyone who knocks, the door will be opened. Is there anyone among you who, if your child asks for bread, will give a stone? Or if the child asks for a fish, will give a snake? If you then, who are evil, know how to give good gifts to your children, how much more will your Father in heaven give good things to those who ask him!"

- Jesus illustrates the Golden Rule, "Do to others as you would have them do to you." The Rabbi Hillel used to say about this: "The rest is commentary. Now go and study."

- I study myself. How do I wish people would treat me? Lord, show me where I fall down on this.

Friday 6th March   Matthew 5:20–26

Jesus said to his disciples, "For I tell you, unless your righteousness exceeds that of the scribes and Pharisees, you will never enter the kingdom of heaven. You have heard that it was said to those of ancient times, 'You shall not murder'; and 'whoever murders shall be liable to judgment.' But I say to you that if you are angry with a brother or sister, you will be liable to judgment;

and if you insult a brother or sister, you will be liable to the council; and if you say, 'You fool,' you will be liable to the hell of fire. So when you are offering your gift at the altar, if you remember that your brother or sister has something against you, leave your gift there before the altar and go; first be reconciled to your brother or sister, and then come and offer your gift. Come to terms quickly with your accuser while you are on the way to court with him, or your accuser may hand you over to the judge, and the judge to the guard, and you will be thrown into prison. Truly I tell you, you will never get out until you have paid the last penny."

- The listeners knew their Bible and the law of Moses. Jesus takes the law and makes it deeper, more interior. The root of the act of killing is in the angry hatred of the killer's heart. Tackle the evil at its source.

- Does that mean that I must repress and deny all anger? You might as well deny feeling hot in the Sahara desert. The feeling is innocent; the evil arises when I act out my anger and injure my neighbour, when I give way to hatred, to anger.

- Lord, I come before your altar. Help me to work on the seeds of hatred in my heart. You tell me that there can be no true worship of God without justice.

Saturday 7th March　　　　**Matthew 5:43–48**

Jesus said to the disciples, "You have heard that it was said, 'You shall love your neighbour and hate your enemy.' But I say to you, Love your enemies and pray for those who persecute you, so that you may be children of your Father in heaven; for he makes his sun rise on the evil and on the good, and sends rain on the righteous and on the unrighteous. For if you love those who love you, what reward do you have? Do not even the tax collectors do the same? And if you greet only your brothers and sisters, what more are you doing than others? Do not even the Gentiles do the same? Be perfect, therefore, as your heavenly Father is perfect."

- Lord, you warn us against tribal or racial exclusiveness, where we love only kith and kin, and reject outsiders. For you there are no outsiders. Your sun shines and your rain falls on all alike. We are to open our hearts even to those who hate us.

- Is this hopeless idealism or a wise strategy for overcoming the persecutor? Teach me to change aggression into a strategy for winning through the wisdom of love.

Something to think and pray about each day this week:

God's dependants

St. Paul tells us that "the body is for the Lord." And so it is—destined to be transfigured like Christ's. But the body is also subject to sin, suffering, and death. Illness or bereavement brings home to us in stark fashion the misery of our human condition while at the same time heightening our nostalgia for the destiny intended for us, eternal life.

Lent is a time to take stock of our true situation, to remember that we are creatures, not gods, and thus utterly dependent on God's gratuitous love and mercy. This should not frighten or dismay us but rather fill us with gratitude for the miracle of salvation that God has wrought in our lives.

"Come, let us bow and do reverence; kneel before Yahweh who made us."

The Presence of God

I pause for a moment
and think of the love and the grace that God
showers on me,
creating me in his image and likeness,
making me his temple.

Freedom

Everything has the potential to draw forth from
me a fuller love and life.
Yet my desires are often fixed, caught,
on illusions of fulfillment.
I ask that God, through my freedom, may
orchestrate
my desires in a vibrant loving melody rich in
harmony.

Consciousness

In the presence of my loving Creator,
I look honestly at my feelings over the last day,

the highs, the lows, and the level ground.
Can I see where the Lord has been present?

The Word

God speaks to each one of us individually. I need
to listen to what he is saying to me. (Please turn
to your scripture on the following pages. Inspiration points are there should you need them.
When you are ready, return here to continue.)

Conversation

What feelings are rising in me
as I pray and reflect on God's Word?
I imagine Jesus himself sitting or standing
beside me,
and open my heart to him.

Conclusion

Glory be to the Father, and to the Son, and
to the Holy Spirit, as it was in the beginning,
is now and ever shall be, World without end.
Amen

Sunday 8th March,
Second Sunday of Lent   Mark 9:2–10

Six days later, Jesus took with him Peter and James and John, and led them up a high mountain apart, by themselves. And he was transfigured before them, and his clothes became dazzling white, such as no one on earth could bleach them. And there appeared to them Elijah with Moses, who were talking with Jesus. Then Peter said to Jesus, "Rabbi, it is good for us to be here; let us make three dwellings, one for you, one for Moses, and one for Elijah." He did not know what to say, for they were terrified. Then a cloud overshadowed them, and from the cloud there came a voice, "This is my Son, the Beloved; listen to him!" Suddenly when they looked around, they saw no one with them any more, but only Jesus. As they were coming down the mountain, he ordered them to tell no one about what they had seen, until after the Son of Man had risen from the dead. So they kept the matter to themselves, questioning what this rising from the dead could mean.

- Imagine yourself to be present at this scene. What is it like? What are Elijah, Moses, and Jesus talking to each other about?

- How do you imagine the voice that says, "This is my Son . . ."?

- At the end of the scene, when Jesus is standing there alone, what do you want to say to him?

Monday 9th March   Luke 6:36–38

Jesus said to the disciples, "Be merciful, just as your Father is merciful. Do not judge, and you will not be judged; do not condemn, and you will not be condemned. Forgive, and you will be forgiven; give, and it will be given to you. A good measure, pressed down, shaken together, running over, will be put into your lap; for the measure you give will be the measure you get back."

- Lord, my lap and my hands are open to receive from you. You tell me they will be able to contain the cascade of good things from your hand, provided my hands are open to give as well as to receive. Can I open my hands? Does my trust have limits?

Tuesday 10th March   Matthew 23:8–12

Jesus said to the crowds and to his disciples, "You are not to be called rabbi, for you have one teacher, and you are all students. And call no one your father on earth, for you have one Father—the one in heaven. Nor are you to be called instructors, for you have one instructor, the Messiah. The greatest among you will be your servant. All who exalt themselves will be humbled, and all who humble themselves will be exalted."

- Do I have the openness and humility to accept instruction, to learn new lessons, or do I exalt myself and think I know it all at this stage?

- Saint Ignatius writes in his autobiography of times in his adult life when God dealt with him "as a schoolteacher deals with a pupil." What lessons might God have to teach me? Would I be listening?

- Can I ask for the grace to be attentive and listening, and to be able to discern what God is trying to tell me?

Wednesday 11th March   Matthew 20:17–23

While Jesus was going up to Jerusalem, he took the twelve disciples aside by themselves, and said to them on the way, "See, we are going up to Jerusalem, and the Son of Man will be handed over to the chief priests and scribes, and they will condemn him to death; then they will hand him over to the Gentiles to be mocked and flogged and crucified; and on the third day he will be raised. Then the mother of the sons of Zebedee came to him with her sons, and kneeling before him, she asked a favor of him. And he said to her, "What do you want?" She said to him, "Declare that these two sons of mine will sit, one at your right hand and one at your left, in your kingdom." But Jesus answered, "You do not know what you are asking. Are you able to drink the cup that I am about to drink?" They said to him, "We are able." He said to them, "You will indeed drink my cup, but to sit at my right hand and at my left, this is not mine to grant, but it is for those for whom it has been prepared by my Father."

- Lord, you listened to the pushy Mrs. Zebedee. Her sons James and John said yes, they could drink from your cup. But when the time for suffering came, James at least went into hiding.

- Among your followers, there is no place for lording it over others. The only dignity lies in being a servant. Am I slow to learn this lesson, Lord? Am I listening?

Thursday 12th March   **Jeremiah 17:5–8**

Thus says the Lord: Cursed are those who trust in mere mortals and make mere flesh their strength, whose hearts turn away from the Lord. They shall be like a shrub in the desert, and shall not see when relief comes. They shall live in the parched places of the wilderness, in an uninhabited salt land. Blessed are those who trust in the Lord, whose trust is the Lord. They shall be like a tree planted by water, sending out its roots by the stream. It shall not fear when heat comes, and its leaves shall stay green; in the year of drought it is not anxious, and it does not cease to bear fruit.

- The one who trusts in the Lord is like a tree planted by water, that sends out its roots to the stream and does not fear when the heat comes. I know, Lord, what dryness, desolation, and sterility feel like. Let me pray with you.

Friday 13th March   Matthew 21:33–43, 45–46

Jesus said: "Listen to another parable. There was a landowner who planted a vineyard, put a fence around it, dug a wine press in it, and built a watchtower. Then he leased it to tenants and went to another country. When the harvest time had come, he sent his slaves to the tenants to collect his produce. But the tenants seized his slaves and beat one, killed another, and stoned another. Again he sent other slaves, more than the first; and they treated them in the same way. Finally he sent his son to them, saying, 'They will respect my son.' But when the tenants saw the son, they said to themselves, 'This is the heir; come, let us kill him and get his inheritance.' So they seized him, threw him out of the vineyard, and killed him. Now when the owner of the vineyard comes, what will he do to those tenants?" They said to him, "He will put those wretches to a miserable death, and lease the vineyard to other tenants who will give him the produce at the harvest time." Jesus said to them, "Have you never read in the scriptures: 'The stone that the builders rejected has become the cornerstone; this was the Lord's doing, and it is amazing in our eyes'? Therefore I tell you, the kingdom of God will be taken away from you and given to a people that produces the fruits of the kingdom." When the chief priests and the Pharisees heard his parables, they realized that he was speaking about them. They wanted to arrest him, but they feared the crowds, because they regarded him as a prophet.

- Lord, this parable is about the Jews, but also about me. I am the tenant of your vineyard. For me you have planted and protected a crop, and from me you expect some harvest.

- The fruit of my labors is for you, not for me. I may feel annoyed when you ask, but you are right to expect something of me.

Saturday 14th March   Micah 7:14–15, 18–20

Shepherd your people with your staff, the flock that belongs to you, which lives alone in a forest in the midst of a garden land; let them feed in Bashan and Gilead as in the days of old. As in the days when you came out of the land of Egypt, show us marvelous things. Who is a God like you, pardoning iniquity and passing over the transgression of the remnant of your possession? He does not retain his anger forever, because he delights in showing clemency. He will again have compassion upon us; he will tread our iniquities under foot. You will cast all our sins into the depths of the sea. You will show faithfulness to Jacob and unswerving loyalty to Abraham, as you have sworn to our ancestors from the days of old.

• He does not retain his anger forever, because he delights in steadfast love. The parable of the prodigal son gives me a picture of that steadfast love. There, Lord, you show how your heavenly father would appear in human form. When he welcomes back his lost son with tears of delight, kills the fatted calf, brings out the best robe, and throws a great party, it is not to please other people, but to give expression to his own overwhelming pleasure that his child has come home. You delight in me.

Something to think and pray about each day this week:

The loving fire of purification

Dante Alighieri's *Inferno* paints an ugly picture of hell's torments. And the author wasn't shy of naming some of his contemporaries who would, by virtue of their behavior, find themselves there! Hyperbole, perhaps, but nevertheless a salutary jolt reminding us all that sparks from hell can and do take root in our hearts, with bilious results! In Galatians, Paul lists them out: antagonisms, rivalry, jealousy, bad temper, quarrels, disagreements, factions, malice. We might do well to review them.

Lent is a time of purification. We resolve to let the fire of love—heaven's spark—clear out any pathogenic toxins (resentment, bitterness, greed, lust, etc.) that reside unchallenged in our system. Like Jesus, we need to clear out the Temple so that love can hold sway over all selfish tendencies.

The Presence of God

I reflect for a moment on God's presence around me and in me.

Creator of the universe, the sun and the moon, the earth,

every molecule, every atom, everything that is:

God is in every beat of my heart.

God is with me, now.

Freedom

A thick and shapeless tree-trunk would never believe

that it could become a statue, admired as a miracle of sculpture,

and would never submit itself to the chisel of the sculptor,

who sees by her genius what she can make of it (St. Ignatius).

I ask for the grace to let myself be shaped by my loving Creator.

Consciousness

Knowing that God loves me unconditionally,
I look honestly over the last day,
its events and my feelings.
Do I have something to be grateful for?
Then I give thanks.
Is there something I am sorry for?
Then I ask forgiveness.

The Word

I read the Word of God slowly, a few times
over, and I listen to what God is saying to me.
(Please turn to your scripture on the following
pages. Inspiration points are there should you
need them. When you are ready, return here to
continue.)

Conversation

What is stirring in me as I pray?
Am I consoled, troubled, left cold?
I imagine Jesus himself standing or sitting at

my side,
and share my feelings with him.

Conclusion

Glory be to the Father, and to the Son, and
to the Holy Spirit, as it was in the beginning,
is now and ever shall be, world without end.
Amen

Sunday 15th March,

Third Sunday of Lent   1 Corinthians 1:25–30

For God's foolishness is wiser than human wisdom, and God's weakness is stronger than human strength. Consider your own call, brothers and sisters: not many of you were wise by human standards, not many were powerful, not many were of noble birth. But God chose what is foolish in the world to shame the wise; God chose what is weak in the world to shame the strong; God chose what is low and despised in the world, things that are not, to reduce to nothing things that are, so that no one might boast in the presence of God. He is the source of your life in Christ Jesus, who became for us wisdom from God, and righteousness and sanctification and redemption.

- You could not ask for a clearer expression of the revolutionary character of Christianity than these lines from St. Paul.

- How do I feel when I read these lines? Inspired? Ashamed? Challenged?

- What might I do differently if I were putting into practice the standard spelled out here?

- What do I really want? To live my life by this standard, or to be "somebody," to be influential and important? Can I talk to the Lord about this?

Monday 16th March   **Luke 4:24–30**

And he said, "Truly I tell you, no prophet is accepted in the prophet's hometown. But the truth is, there were many widows in Israel in the time of Elijah, when the heaven was shut up three years and six months, and there was a severe famine over all the land; yet Elijah was sent to none of them except to a widow at Zarephath in Sidon. There were also many lepers in Israel in the time of the prophet Elisha, and none of them was cleansed except Naaman the Syrian." When they heard this, all in the synagogue were filled with rage. They got up, drove him out of the town, and led him to the brow of the hill on which their town was built, so that they might hurl him off the cliff. But he passed through the midst of them and went on his way.

- Jesus, speaking to his Jewish neighbors in Nazareth, is pointing to instances of God reaching out to the Gentiles, and the listeners are furious.

- How we cherish this illusion that we are the center of the universe, and that outsiders do not count! Unblinker me, Lord.

Tuesday 17th March,
St. Patrick   Isaiah 52:7–10

How beautiful upon the mountains are the feet of the messenger who announces peace, who brings good news, who announces salvation, who says to Zion, "Your God reigns." Listen! Your sentinels lift up their voices, together they sing for joy; for in plain sight they see the return of the Lord to Zion. Break forth together into singing, you ruins of Jerusalem; for the Lord has comforted his people, he has redeemed Jerusalem. The Lord has bared his holy arm before the eyes of all the nations; and all the ends of the earth shall see the salvation of our God.

• As a teenager, St. Patrick was kidnapped and lived the life of a slave herding swine on a hillside. In that isolation he turned to God in prayer; that was his nourishment and protection. He left us *The Deer's Cry*:

Christ as a light, illumine and guide me.
Christ as a shield, o'ershadow and cover me.
Christ be under me, Christ be over me,
Christ be beside me, on left hand and right.
Christ be before me, behind me, around me.
Christ this day be within and without me.
Amen.

Wednesday 18th March   Matthew 5:17–19

Do not think that I have come to abolish the law or the prophets; I have come not to abolish but to fulfill. For truly I tell you, until heaven and earth pass away, not one letter, not one stroke of a letter, will pass from the law until all is accomplished. Therefore, whoever breaks one of the least of these commandments, and teaches others to do the same, will be called least in the kingdom of heaven; but whoever does them and teaches them will be called great in the kingdom of heaven.

- Jesus did not reject the Old Testament of the Jews, but brought it back to its basics: love God and love your neighbor.

- It is harder to live one sermon than to preach a dozen. Lord, help me to make my life whole, so that other people learn Christian principles from my behavior.

Thursday 19th March,
St. Joseph   Matthew 1:18–25

Now the birth of Jesus the Messiah took place in this way. When his mother Mary had been engaged to Joseph, but before they lived together, she was found to be with child from the Holy Spirit. Her husband Joseph, being a righteous man and unwilling to expose her to public disgrace, planned to dismiss her quietly. But just when he had resolved to do this, an angel of the Lord appeared to him in a dream and said, "Joseph, son of David, do not be afraid

to take Mary as your wife, for the child con-
ceived in her is from the Holy Spirit. She will
bear a son, and you are to name him Jesus, for
he will save his people from their sins." All this
took place to fulfill what had been spoken by
the Lord through the prophet: "Look, the virgin shall conceive and bear a son, and they shall
name him Emmanuel," which means, "God is
with us." When Joseph awoke from sleep, he
did as the angel of the Lord commanded him;
he took her as his wife, but had no marital rela-
tions with her until she had borne a son; and he
named him Jesus.

- How do we think about St. Joseph? Yes, he receives the news of the Annunciation, and he is
  there with Mary during her pregnancy and the
  birth of Jesus. But he is also the man working to
  support his family for many years, providing guid-
  ance, education and example to the young Jesus.

- Can I imagine the everyday life of Joseph, with the young Jesus trailing behind him, copying his actions, listening carefully to what he said? What did Joseph observe in this growing boy? What glimpses of the future did he see?

Friday 20th March   Mark 12:28–34

One of the scribes came near and heard them disputing with one another, and seeing that he answered them well, he asked him, "Which commandment is the first of all?" Jesus answered, "The first is, 'Hear, O Israel: the Lord our God, the Lord is one; you shall love the Lord your God with all your heart, and with all your soul, and with all your mind, and with all your strength.' The second is this, 'You shall love your neighbor as yourself.' There is no other commandment greater than these." Then the scribe said to him, "You are right, Teacher; you have truly said that 'he is one, and besides

him there is no other'; and 'to love him with all
the heart, and with all the understanding, and
with all the strength,' and 'to love one's neighbor as oneself,'—this is much more important
than all whole burnt offerings and sacrifices."
When Jesus saw that he answered wisely, he said
to him, "You are not far from the kingdom of
God." After that no one dared to ask him any
question.

• "The Lord our God, the Lord is one." As I hear
  Jesus' answer to the scribe, I think how a Muslim
  would agree warmly with all that he hears, and
  how Jesus might well say of many a Muslim, Jew,
  and Christian equally: "You are not far from the
  kingdom of God." Lord, let me not put barriers
  where you put windows.

Saturday 21st March   **Luke 18:9–14**

He also told this parable to some who trusted
in themselves that they were righteous and

regarded others with contempt: "Two men went up to the Temple to pray, one a Pharisee and the other a tax collector. The Pharisee, standing by himself, was praying thus, 'God, I thank you that I am not like other people: thieves, rogues, adulterers, or even like this tax collector. I fast twice a week; I give a tenth of all my income.' But the tax collector, standing far off, would not even look up to heaven, but was beating his breast and saying, 'God, be merciful to me, a sinner!' I tell you, this man went down to his home justified rather than the other; for all who exalt themselves will be humbled, but all who humble themselves will be exalted."

- The contrast between Pharisee and tax collector has entered so deeply into our culture; Pharisee, a term of honor in Jesus' society, is not something we want to be called today. To place it in our culture, read convicted rapist, pedophile, tyrant; any hate-figure of the popular press. We are sometimes persuaded to despise them as the Pharisee despised the humble tax-collector. It is not for us to look down on anyone.

• How does the story hit me? I fear being an object of people's contempt. But Lord, if they knew me as you do, they might be right to feel contempt. I have no right to look down on those whose sins are paraded in the media. Be merciful to me.

Something to think and pray about each day this week:

The sense of God's love

"Then he came to his senses." This deceptively simple statement about the prodigal son poses a profound challenge to us all. None of us can claim to be without sin. "We all fall short of the glory of God." Lent can be that moment in which we come to our senses, face facts about ourselves, and make the appropriate adjustments.

After a brief romantic affair which threatened to destroy his marriage and alienate his family and friends, John came to his senses. Before matters got worse, he had the courage to face his fault, admit his sin, and turn back. He was fortunate to receive his wife's understanding, love, and forgiveness.

During Lent we turn back to God and entrust ourselves once again to his immense mercy. We allow the Father to embrace us in our sinfulness and sorrow. In being forgiven much, we discover the depths of God's love.

The Presence of God

In the silence of my innermost being,
in the fragments of my yearned-for wholeness,
can I hear the whispers of God's presence?
Can I remember when I felt God's nearness?
When we walked together and I let myself be
embraced by God's love.

Freedom

There are very few people
who realize what God would make of them
if they abandoned themselves into his hands,
and let themselves be formed by his grace
(St. Ignatius).
I ask for the grace to trust myself totally to
God's love.

Consciousness

How do I find myself today?
Where am I with God? With others?
Do I have something to be grateful for?

march 2009

Then I give thanks.
Is there something I am sorry for?
Then I ask forgiveness.

The Word

I take my time to read the Word of God, slowly,
a few times, allowing myself to dwell on any-
thing that strikes me. (Please turn to your scripture on the following pages. Inspiration points
are there should you need them. When you are
ready, return here to continue.)

Conversation

Do I notice myself reacting as I pray with the
Word of God?
Do I feel challenged, comforted, angry?
Imagining Jesus sitting or standing by me,
I speak out my feelings,
as one trusted friend to another.

Conclusion

Glory be to the Father, and to the Son, and to the Holy Spirit, as it was in the beginning, is now and ever shall be, World without end. Amen

Sunday 22nd March,
Fourth Sunday of Lent   John 3:14–18

Jesus said to Nicodemus, "And just as Moses lifted up the serpent in the wilderness, so must the Son of Man be lifted up, that whoever believes in him may have eternal life. For God so loved the world that he gave his only Son, so that everyone who believes in him may not perish but may have eternal life. Indeed, God did not send the Son into the world to condemn the world, but in order that the world might be saved through him. Those who believe in him are not condemned; but those who do not believe are condemned already, because they have not believed in the name of the only Son of God."

• With Moses in the desert, the people looked up at the serpent and were healed. Jesus wants me to look up at him and be healed.

- Our lives are serious and can go very badly wrong. In the times of greatest chaos the Son is there for me.

- Can I open my heart to accept that all God's love is there for me?

Monday 23rd March   John 4:46b–54

Now there was a royal official whose son lay ill in Capernaum. When he heard that Jesus had come from Judea to Galilee, he went and begged him to come down and heal his son, for he was at the point of death. Then Jesus said to him, "Unless you see signs and wonders you will not believe." The official said to him, "Sir, come down before my little boy dies." Jesus said to him, "Go; your son will live." The man believed the word that Jesus spoke to him and started on his way. As he was going down, his slaves met him and told him that his child was alive. So he asked them the hour when he began to recover, and they said to him, "Yesterday at one in the afternoon the fever left him." The father realized that this was the hour when Jesus had said to him, "Your son will live." So he himself believed, along with his whole household. Now this was the second sign that Jesus did after coming from Judea to Galilee.

- At first Jesus recoils; what he treasures is the company of those who want to know God for himself, not for what he can deliver. The father returns as a believer, and Jesus welcomes him.

- Lord, forgive me for the times I have turned to you in a crisis, begging a favor. When the crisis passes, I go back to living as though you did not exist. I want to find time for you.

Tuesday 24th March   John 5:1–8

After this there was a festival of the Jews, and Jesus went up to Jerusalem. Now in Jerusalem by the Sheep Gate there is a pool, called in Hebrew Beth-zatha, which has five porticoes. In these lay many invalids—blind, lame, and paralyzed. One man was there who had been ill for thirty-eight years. When Jesus saw him lying there and knew that he had been there a long time, he said to him, "Do you want to be made well?" The sick man answered him, "Sir, I have no one to put me into the pool when the water is stirred up; and while I am making my way, someone else steps down ahead of me." Jesus said to him, "Stand up, take your mat and walk."

- Jesus asks the crippled man a curious question: "Do you want to be healed?" Surely that much was obvious.

- But the question does makes sense, if a cure would change his life and push him back into the daily grind. If sickness becomes a way of life, it is hard to face this change. Save me, Lord, from making excuses, from pleading my special circumstances.

Wednesday 25th March,
The Annunciation   Luke 1:26–32, 34–35, 38a

In the sixth month the angel Gabriel was sent by God to a town in Galilee called Nazareth, to a virgin engaged to a man whose name was Joseph, of the house of David. The virgin's name was Mary. And he came to her and said, "Greetings, favored one! The Lord is with you." But she was much perplexed by his words and pondered what sort of greeting this might be. The angel said to her, "Do not be afraid, Mary, for you have found favor with God. And now, you will conceive in your womb and bear a son, and you will name him Jesus. He will be great, and will be called the Son of the Most High, and the Lord God will give to him the throne of his ancestor David." Mary said to the angel, "How can this be, since I am a virgin?" The angel said to her, "The Holy Spirit will come upon you, and the power of the Most High will overshadow you; therefore the child to be born will be holy; he will be called Son of God." Then Mary said, "Here am I, the servant of the Lord; let it be with me according to your word."

- You might find it helpful to contemplate a picture of this scene.

- Imagine what Mary felt as she was given this awesome news.

- Mary has questions and she voices them, but she says "Yes" to God's will for her. Can I learn from her example?

Thursday 26th March   John 5:44–47

Jesus said to the Jews, "How can you believe when you accept glory from one another and do not seek the glory that comes from the one who alone is God? Do not think that I will accuse you before the Father; your accuser is Moses, on whom you have set your hope. If you believed Moses, you would believe me, for he wrote about me. But if you do not believe what he wrote, how will you believe what I say?"

- This reading reflects the age-old struggle between God and his chosen people, the Jews. It says something to us too: "How can you believe, who receive glory from one another, and do not seek the glory that comes from the only God?"

- Lord, I often hunger for an ego massage, for the good feeling when other people accept and approve of me. Do I make too much of it? Does it turn me from seeking you?

Friday 27th March   **Wisdom 2:1, 12–15**

For the godless reasoned unsoundly, saying to themselves, "Short and sorrowful is our life, and there is no remedy when a life comes to its end, and no one has been known to return from Hades. Let us lie in wait for the righteous man, because he is inconvenient to us and opposes our actions; he reproaches us for sins against the law, and accuses us of sins against our training. He professes to have knowledge of God, and calls himself a child of the Lord. He became to us a reproof of our thoughts; the very sight of him is a burden to us, because his manner of life is unlike that of others, and his ways are strange."

• You touch me where it hurts, Lord, when you describe the jealousy we often feel for somebody whose life is different and pulls us up sharply. "He became to us a reproof of our thoughts; the very sight of him is a burden to us."

• Do we ever get over sibling rivalry? It is a sign of grace to be happy at the sight of somebody close to us who outshines us, whether in conversation, friendship, or work. Lord, make my heart more generous, so that I rejoice in the success of others.

Saturday 28th March John 7:50–53

Nicodemus, who had gone to Jesus before, and who was one of the Pharisees, asked, "Our law does not judge people without first giving them a hearing to find out what they are doing, does it?" They replied, "Surely you are not also from Galilee, are you? Search and you will see that no prophet is to arise from Galilee." Then each of them went home.

- They went each to his own house. They retreated to safety; at their own table they would not face disagreement, there they could indulge their prejudices at will.

- Lord, I do it myself; I turn away from people with different viewpoints, I do not engage with them, but retreat into the company of those who share my prejudices. Give me the blessed gift of listening and answering, especially when I am feeling uncomfortable.

Something to think and pray about each day this week:

Seeing the real Jesus

Jesus excited curiosity so that people like Zacchaeus (Luke 19:1) and Greek visitors to the festival (John 12:20) wanted to see him, to know what he looked like.

But Jesus had other ideas, confronting and revolutionary ideas. To "see" him was to enter totally into his way of thinking, to understand why he had to suffer and die and rise again. Like the grain of wheat, Jesus has to let go of everything, including his own life, in order to bring life to himself and many others. This is the "emptying," the *kenosis*, that the Letter to the Philippians speaks about. In the process, Jesus and we will be transformed, just as the grain of wheat, apparently annihilated, becomes something altogether greater and enriching for others.

Are we ready for that? Are we afraid to let everything go? Is Jesus asking too much? Lead us to see and accept this as the core of Jesus' life, so that we really see him.

The Presence of God

I remind myself that, as I sit here now,
God is gazing on me with love and holding me
in being.
I pause for a moment and think of this.

Freedom

I ask for the grace
to let go of my own concerns
and be open to what God is asking of me,
to let myself be guided and formed
by my loving Creator.

Consciousness

In God's loving presence I unwind the past day,
starting from now and looking back, moment
by moment.
I gather in all the goodness and light, in gratitude.
I attend to the shadows and what they say to me,
seeking healing, courage, forgiveness.

The Word

God speaks to each one of us individually.
I need to listen to what he is saying to me.
(Please turn to your scripture on the following
pages. Inspiration points are there should you
need them. When you are ready, return here to
continue.)

Conversation

Remembering that I am still in God's presence,
I imagine Jesus himself standing or sitting
beside me,
and say whatever is on my mind,
whatever is in my heart,
speaking as one friend to another.

Conclusion

Glory be to the Father, and to the Son, and
to the Holy Spirit, as it was in the beginning,
is now and ever shall be, world without end.
Amen

Sunday 29th March,
Fifth Sunday of Lent John 12:20–24

Now among those who went up to worship at the festival were some Greeks. They came to Philip, who was from Bethsaida in Galilee, and said to him, "Sir, we wish to see Jesus." Philip went and told Andrew; then Andrew and Philip went and told Jesus. Jesus answered them, "The hour has come for the Son of Man to be glorified. Very truly, I tell you, unless a grain of wheat falls into the earth and dies, it remains just a single grain; but if it dies, it bears much fruit."

- Imagine the scene. Some Greeks, complete newcomers, went to meet Jesus. What attracted them?

- They immediately hear ominous predictions about suffering and death. We don't even know if they understood or were frightened off.

- How do I react to Jesus' talk of coming trials?

- Remember that I am told these things not to frighten me but to strengthen me.

Monday 30th March Daniel 13:55–56, 60–62

Daniel said, "Indeed! Your lie recoils on you own head: the angel of God has already received from him your sentence and will cut you in half." He dismissed the man, ordered the other to be brought and said to him, "Son of Canaan, not of Judah, beauty has seduced you, lust has led your heart astray!" . . . Then the whole assembly shouted, blessing God, the Saviour of those who trust in him. And they turned on the two elders whom Daniel had convicted of false evidence out of their own mouths. As the Law of Moses prescribes, they were given the same punishment as they had schemed to inflict on their neighbour. They were put to death. And thus, that day, an innocent life was saved.

- These are not happy characters. Dissipation and addiction are forms of imprisonment in which the chains are inside you, not outside, so the pain is greater. The German ("God is dead") philosopher Nietzsche stated the downside of lust: "The mother of dissipation is not joy, but joylessness." Thomas Aquinas put it more positively: "A joyful heart is a sure sign of temperance and self-control." Do I show that sign?

Tuesday 31st March   Numbers 21:4–9

From Mount Hor they set out by the way to the Red Sea, to go around the land of Edom; but the people became impatient on the way. The people spoke against God and against Moses, "Why have you brought us up out of Egypt to die in the wilderness? For there is no food and no water, and we detest this miserable food." Then the Lord sent poisonous serpents among the people, and they bit the people, so that many

Israelites died. The people came to Moses and said, "We have sinned by speaking against the Lord and against you; pray to the Lord to take away the serpents from us." So Moses prayed for the people. And the Lord said to Moses, "Make a poisonous serpent, and set it on a pole; and everyone who is bitten shall look at it and live." So Moses made a serpent of bronze, and put it upon a pole; and whenever a serpent bit someone, that person would look at the serpent of bronze and live.

- The Book of Numbers tells a story of people complaining, being punished, turning to God, and finding relief.

- Lord, you have often taught me like a strict parent, and when I look back on the periods of punishment, they sometimes brought me greater blessings and wisdom than times of consolation.

You lead me to more abundant life through pruning and pain.

Wednesday 1st April — John 8:31–32

Then Jesus said to the Jews who had believed in him, "If you continue in my word, you are truly my disciples; and you will know the truth, and the truth will make you free."

- "The truth will make you free." But at a cost. The man who acknowledges that he cannot control his drinking, the mother who admits that her darling son is a bully at school, the girl who accepts that her shoplifting is a form of stealing, they are all liberated by seeing the truth, but they have to pay a price.

- Are there issues in my life which I fear to face, where I dodge the truth? Who can tell me the truth—my friends, or my enemies? It is often the remarks that rankle with us that push us to face unwelcome truths.

Thursday 2nd April   **Genesis 17:3–8**

T hen Abram fell on his face; and God said to him, "As for me, this is my covenant with you: You shall be the ancestor of a multitude of nations. No longer shall your name be Abram, but your name shall be Abraham; for I have made you the ancestor of a multitude of nations. I will make you exceedingly fruitful; and I will make nations of you, and kings shall come from you. I will establish my covenant between me and you, and your offspring after you throughout their generations, for an everlasting covenant, to be God to you and to your offspring after you. And I will give to you, and to your offspring after you, the land where you are now an alien, all the land of Canaan, for a perpetual holding; and I will be their God."

- God made a covenant with Abraham. What sort of special choosing, planning, and missioning is that?

- The covenant was not just for an individual. It is meant to embrace and involve a great community.

- How does God's covenant with humankind embrace and engage me?

Friday 3rd April   Psalm 18:1–3

I love you, O Lord, my strength. The Lord is my rock, my fortress, and my deliverer, my God, my rock in whom I take refuge, my shield, and the horn of my salvation, my stronghold. I call upon the Lord, who is worthy to be praised, so I shall be saved from my enemies.

- The author of the Psalms knew good times and bad. In my own situation can I make these words my own?

Saturday 4th April   **Ezekiel 37:26–28**

I will make a covenant of peace with them; it shall be an everlasting covenant with them; and I will bless them and multiply them, and will set my sanctuary among them forevermore. My dwelling place shall be with them; and I will be their God, and they shall be my people. Then the nations shall know that I the Lord sanctify Israel, when my sanctuary is among them forevermore.

• This is the renewal of God's loving plan with a people who have abandoned and betrayed him.

• There is a plan for my good no matter what has happened.

• What does this say to me?

april 5–11

Something to think and pray about each day this week:

Forsaken, yet transformed

"My God, my God, why have you forsaken me?" This cry of almost total desperation rings out across the centuries from the very bowels of suffering humanity. In our own time, we have witnessed the agony of innocent people's lives blown apart by terrorist bombs. We have seen the tortured faces of the wounded and bereaved on our television screens. God's Kingdom of justice, love, and peace can seem totally remote and meaningless—just a pipe dream. And yet the one who seems "forsaken" says that God is not indifferent. The God-Man Jesus absorbs and embraces all human suffering and transforms it into an act of love. His—and our—forsakenness is not the last word. By divine alchemy, on Calvary, all human suffering is transformed into love.

During this week our *Sacred Space* brings us to the foot of the Cross. As we hear once again Christ's words, "Why have you forsaken me?" we may be drawn to pray with and for the countless women and men who continue to cry out for an explanation, a meaning, for their suffering. We may begin to understand the suffering in our own lives.

The Presence of God

God is with me, but more,
God is within me, giving me existence.
Let me dwell for a moment on God's life-giving
presence
in my body, my mind, my heart
and in the whole of my life.

Freedom

I ask for the grace to believe
in what I could be and do
if I only allowed God, my loving Creator,
to continue to create me, guide me, and
shape me.

Consciousness

I exist in a web of relationships,
links to nature, people, God.
I trace out these links, giving thanks for the life
that flows through them.
Some links are twisted or broken:

I may feel
regret, anger, disappointment.
I pray for the gift of acceptance and forgiveness.

The Word

I read the Word of God slowly, a few times
over, and I listen to what God is saying to me.
(Please turn to your scripture on the following
pages. Inspiration points are there should you
need them. When you are ready, return here to
continue.)

Conversation

How has God's Word moved me?
Has it left me cold?
Has it consoled me or moved me to act in a
new way?
I imagine Jesus standing or sitting beside me,
I turn and share my feelings with him.

Conclusion

Glory be to the Father, and to the Son, and
to the Holy Spirit, as it was in the beginning,
is now and ever shall be, world without end.
Amen

Sunday 5th April, Palm Sunday
of the Lord's Passion   Philippians 2:6–11

Let the same mind be in you that was in Christ Jesus, who, though he was in the form of God, did not regard equality with God as something to be exploited, but emptied himself, taking the form of a slave, being born in human likeness. And being found in human form, he humbled himself and became obedient to the point of death—even death on a cross. Therefore God also highly exalted him and gave him the name that is above every name, so that at the name of Jesus every knee should bend, in heaven and on earth and under the earth, and every tongue should confess that Jesus Christ is Lord, to the glory of God the Father.

- Lord, give me the grace to celebrate this occasion. Palm Sunday did not last—what does? But while we dance together, it is a foretaste of heaven.

Monday 6th April   Isaiah 42:1–4

Here is my servant, whom I uphold, my chosen, in whom my soul delights; I have put my spirit upon him; he will bring forth justice to the nations. He will not cry or lift up his voice, or make it heard in the street; a bruised reed he will not break, and a dimly burning wick he will not quench; he will faithfully bring forth justice. He will not grow faint or be crushed until he has established justice in the earth; and the coastlands wait for his teaching.

- "My servant will not cry or lift up his voice, or make it heard in the street . . . he will faithfully bring forth justice."

- That is our mission too, Lord: not by force or violence, but by gentle, faithful persistence, to bring forth justice on the earth.

Tuesday 7th April   **Isaiah 49:1–4**

Listen to me, O coastlands, pay attention, you peoples from far away! The Lord called me before I was born, while I was in my mother's womb he named me. He made my mouth like a sharp sword, in the shadow of his hand he hid me; he made me a polished arrow, in his quiver he hid me away. And he said to me, "You are my servant, Israel, in whom I will be glorified." But I said, "I have labored in vain, I have spent my strength for nothing and vanity; yet surely my cause is with the Lord, and my reward with my God."

- God knows me intimately, even from my first moments. He has a plan for me; whatever talents I have he can put to use.

- Do I stand in the Lord's way, with my own plan? I worked hard, I tried my best but now I have nothing left to give. Is this now the Lord's time when my way seems blocked?

Wednesday 8th April　　　Matthew 26:14–16

T hen one of the twelve, who was called Judas Iscariot, went to the chief priests and said, "What will you give me if I betray him to you?" They paid him thirty pieces of silver. And from that moment he began to look for an opportunity to betray him.

- There were two treacheries. Judas went out to grab his money, betrayed Jesus, and then killed himself in despair. Peter, despite his protests, would deny his Lord; he faced his own appalling guilt, then wept bitterly. His failure was not the end of his mission, but the beginning.

- Success is what I do with my failures. Teach me to trust in your love Lord, no matter what I have done, and to learn from my mistakes and even from treachery.

Thursday 9th April,
Holy Thursday   John 13:12–16

After Jesus had washed their feet, had put on his robe, and had returned to the table, he said to them, "Do you know what I have done to you? You call me Teacher and Lord—and you are right, for that is what I am. So if I, your Lord and Teacher, have washed your feet, you also ought to wash one another's feet. For I have set you an example, that you also should do as I have done to you. Very truly, I tell you, servants are not greater than their master, nor are messengers greater than the one who sent them."

- John's gospel describes the Last Supper without mentioning the Eucharist. Instead it describes Jesus washing his friends' feet.

- On his knees like a servant, Jesus turned human status upside down. Do I celebrate with the community of those who serve?

Friday 10th April,
Good Friday Isaiah 53:1–5

Who has believed what we have heard? And to whom has the arm of the Lord been revealed? For he grew up before him like a young plant, and like a root out of dry ground; he had no form or majesty that we should look at him, nothing in his appearance that we should desire him. He was despised and rejected by others; a man of suffering and acquainted with infirmity; and as one from whom others hide their faces he was despised, and we held him of no account. Surely he has borne our infirmities and carried our diseases; yet we accounted him stricken, struck down by God, and afflicted. But he was wounded for our transgressions, crushed for our iniquities; upon him was the punishment that made us whole, and by his bruises we are healed.

- Now we are at the heart of Jesus' mission: to suffer appallingly and to die without faltering in his love for us. This is where the gospel begins and ends. Yet it is hard to contemplate. We shy away from the pain and injustice of the passion.

- I carry the nail marks in my hands from baptism. I may wander far from the cross, but at the end I am drawn back to it.

Saturday 11th April,
Holy Saturday   Romans 6:3–11

Do you not know that all of us who have been baptized into Christ Jesus were baptized into his death? Therefore we have been buried with him by baptism into death, so that, just as Christ was raised from the dead by the glory of the Father, so we too might walk in newness of life. For if we have been united with him in a death like his, we will certainly be united with him in a resurrection like his. We know that our old self was crucified with him so that the body of sin might be destroyed, and we might no longer be enslaved to sin. For whoever has died is freed from sin. But if we have died with Christ, we believe that we will also live with him. We know that Christ, being raised from the dead, will never die again; death no longer has dominion over him. The death he died, he died to sin, once for all; but the life he lives, he lives to God. So you also must consider yourselves dead to sin and alive to God in Christ Jesus.

- Tonight we reaffirm our ancient faith: Christ has robbed death of its ultimate sting and has invigorated this sweet, precious, precarious, once-only life that is slipping away from us with every hour and day and year.

- When we breathe the evening air, when we catch the sweet smells of the new season, we have hints of a day that knows no ending, a light that will not yield to darkness, and a life in these weary bodies that even creeping death will not be able to frustrate or despoil. We yearn for new life.

april 12

Something to think and pray about each day this week:

The consolation of the Risen Christ

St. Ignatius says that the Risen Christ comes to us first of all as a "Consoler." On that first Easter morning, he appeared to his friends who were still reeling from the ordeal of his passion and death and brought them unimagined consolation and joy.

In these Easter days, can I allow Jesus to come close enough to me to be my Consoler in any sorrow that I experience? Am I open to being a consoler for others?

His consolation, of course, is not a warm fuzzy feeling, but a deep trust in God's love, which is a gift of the Spirit. With that deep consolation I will be able to be a true consoler of others in my turn. As I pray in *Sacred Space* in these days, let me be open to receive this wonderful Easter gift.

The Presence of God

To be present is to arrive as one is and open up
to the other.
At this instant, as I arrive here, God is present,
waiting for me.
God always arrives before me,
desiring to connect with me
even more than my most intimate friend.
I take a moment and greet my loving God.

Freedom

"In these days, God taught me
as a schoolteacher teaches a pupil" (St. Ignatius).
I remind myself that there are things God has to
teach me yet,
and ask for the grace to hear them and let them
change me.

Consciousness

How am I really feeling?
Light-hearted? Heavy-hearted?

I may be very much at peace, happy to be here.
Equally, I may be frustrated, worried, or angry.
I acknowledge how I really am.
It is the real me that the Lord loves.

The Word

I take my time to read the Word of God, slowly,
a few times, allowing myself to dwell on any-
thing that strikes me. (Please turn to your scripture on the following pages. Inspiration points
are there should you need them. When you are
ready, return here to continue.)

Conversation

What feelings are rising in me
as I pray and reflect on God's Word?
I imagine Jesus himself sitting or standing
beside me,
and open my heart to him.

Conclusion

Glory be to the Father, and to the Son, and
to the Holy Spirit, as it was in the beginning,
is now and ever shall be, world without end.
Amen

Sunday 12th April,
Easter Sunday   John 20:1–9

Early on the first day of the week, while it was still dark, Mary Magdalene came to the tomb and saw that the stone had been removed from the tomb. So she ran and went to Simon Peter and the other disciple, the one whom Jesus loved, and said to them, "They have taken the Lord out of the tomb, and we do not know where they have laid him." Then Peter and the other disciple set out and went toward the tomb. The two were running together, but the other disciple outran Peter and reached the tomb first. He bent down to look in and saw the linen wrappings lying there, but he did not go in. Then Simon Peter came, following him, and went into the tomb. He saw the linen wrappings lying there, and the cloth that had been on Jesus' head, not lying with the linen wrappings but rolled up in a place by itself. Then the other disciple, who reached the tomb first, also went in, and he saw and believed; for as yet they did not understand the scripture, that he must rise from the dead.

- Jesus has risen, and we have risen with him to new life.

- Where do I seek him now?

Pre-Order for 2010

The Sacred Space series, inspired by the very popular, successful and interactive website, www.sacredspace.ie, offers a way to reflect and pray each day of the year.

DON'T MISS A DAY!

Sacred Space for Advent and the Christmas Season 2009-2010

ISBN: 9781594711930 / 96 pages

Sacred Space The Prayer Book 2010

ISBN: 9781594711947 / 384 pages

Sacred Space for Lent 2010

ISBN: 9781594711954 / 128 pages

TO PRE-ORDER:

Call: 1.800.282.1865 • Email: avemariapress.1@nd.edu